KV-638-911

Parsons Green Primary Library

In the Snow   05738

First Sports Science

In the
Snow

Nikki Bundey

A *ZOË BOOK*

A ZOË BOOK

© 1997 Zoë Books Limited

Devised and produced by
Zoë Books Limited
15 Worthy Lane
Winchester
Hampshire SO23 7AB
England

Apart from any fair dealing for the purposes of research or private study, or criticism or review, as permitted under the Copyright, Designs and Patents Act, 1988, this publication may only be reproduced, stored or transmitted, in any form or by any means, with the prior permission in writing of the publishers, or in the case of reprographic reproduction in accordance with the terms of licences issued by the Copyright Licensing Agency.

Any person who does any unauthorised act in relation to this publication may be liable to criminal prosecution and civil claims for damages.

First published in Great Britain in 1997 by
Zoë Books Limited
15 Worthy Lane
Winchester
Hampshire SO23 7AB

A record of the CIP data is available from the British Library.

ISBN 1 86173 007 1

Printed in Italy by Grafedit SpA
Editor: Kath Davies
Design & Production: Sterling Associates
Illustrations: Virginia Gray

Photographic acknowledgments

The publishers wish to acknowledge, with thanks, the following photographic sources:

Anton Want 18t / Allsport; 4t / Robert Harding Picture Library; Ken Graham - cover (background), 6b, 8t, 14t / Simon Shepheard 7 / Impact Photos; John Cleare 10b / Mountain Camera; Laurie Campbell 9 / NHPA; J.P.Paireault 5 / Pressens Bild AB 16t / Frank Spooner Pictures; 13b, 19b, 20, 21, 22b, 24t, 25 / Sporting Pictures (U.K.); J.T.Turner - title page, 22t / Telegraph Colour Library; cover (inset, br), 4b, 6t, 8b, 10t, 11, 13t, 14b, 15, 17, 18b, 24b, 26, 27, 28t & b / Zefa.

The publishers have made every effort to trace the copyright holders, but if they have inadvertently overlooked any, they will be pleased to make the necessary arrangement at the first opportunity.

Contents

All the words that appear in **bold** are explained in Words we use on page 30.

In the cold

How cold is it today? You can measure cold with a **thermometer**. Read off the **temperature** it shows. Different **scales** are used to measure temperature. On the Celsius (C) scale, water **freezes** at 0°. It turns to ice.

When water changes into ice, it turns from a **liquid** into a **solid**. This ice has been carved into a slide at an ice festival in Japan. What would happen to the slide if the temperature became warmer?

When the weather is very cold, the water in rivers and lakes freezes over. Ice is hard, cold and slippery to touch.

Snowflakes are made up of beautiful ice **crystals**. They form six sides or points. Every crystal is different.

Water exists in different forms. It is **vapour** in the air we breathe. When air cools, the vapour turns into droplets of water. The drops fall to the ground as rain.

At low temperatures, the water in the air may freeze. It falls as **sleet**, **hail** or snow.

Many sports take place on ice and snow. These skaters are taking part in a race over a frozen river in the Netherlands.

Slipping and sliding

Winter snowstorms can cause chaos as cars skid around and bump into each other. But many children and winter sports fans welcome the snow and ice because they like sliding around!

You need crunchy snow to build a good snowman like this one. To make the body, start with a snowball. As you roll it around, new snow will stick to the snowball. The ice crystals will lock firmly together.

Snow can be cold, wet, hard or powdery, slushy or crunchy. Like ice, it is very slippery.

Young animals like these polar bear cubs enjoy sliding on snow and ice. It is fun and helps them to learn to balance.

When two materials rub against each other, it is called **friction**. Rough materials, such as car tyres on a road, catch at each other. They slow down movement. **Skis** have smooth surfaces. They slide smoothly and quickly over snow with little friction.

Horses can be used to pull **sleighs** across snow. Long ago, people found that they could make all sorts of skis and sleighs with **runners** to carry themselves and their goods over snowy and icy ground.

Safety first!

Snow and ice are fun, but they can be dangerous too. They are so slippery that it is easy to fall over and break an arm or a leg.

Never go on to a frozen pond or river unless it is has been officially passed as safe. Thin ice can easily break and trap you underwater.

Skiing is a dangerous sport. You must learn how to move properly on your skis or you may have an accident.

An **avalanche** roars down the side of a mountain. Great slides of melting snow and rocks can bury people and houses. People who do winter sports in the mountains have to check the weather conditions carefully.

Here are some safety rules.

- Make sure grown-ups know where you are and what you are doing.

- Always carry warm and waterproof clothing with you. Change out of wet clothing as soon as possible.

- On sunny days in the mountains, wear **sun-block** cream to protect your skin. The light off the snow can be dazzling, so wear sunglasses to protect your eyes.

- Obey public warnings about ice and weather conditions.

- Know what to do in an emergency. Don't try to rescue somebody who's in trouble. Know how to use a telephone and get help.

This ice may be strong enough for a duck, but not for a person. If someone falls in, don't try to rescue them. You may fall in too. Fetch help at once.

Wrap up warm

Snow and ice are bitterly cold and high winds can make them even colder. Your body needs to stay warm to survive. If your body's temperature drops too low, it cannot work properly. Extreme cold can damage your skin, crack your lips and even give you **frostbite**.

Clothes help to stop the body from losing heat. They also shield the skin from wind. People used to wear furs to protect them from the cold. Many modern clothes are made from **artificial** materials.

Before you go out to play in the snow, remember – wrap up to keep warm.

If your body temperature drops too low, you will develop **hypothermia**. This blanket is specially designed to hold in warmth to help the victim recover.

Clothes for winter sports must be light and comfortable, as well as warm and waterproof. Skiers and speed-skaters often wear close-fitting, **streamlined** clothes. Clothes which flap or are bulky will drag at the air and slow down the body.

This skier's clothes are made for speed and warmth. The streamlined helmet will protect his head if he falls.

Get fit!

Winter sports keep us strong and fit. Exercise makes the heart work well, pumping blood around the body. The blood passes through the lungs. There, it takes in **oxygen** from the air we breathe.

Skating and skiing can be very fast sports which use a lot of **energy**. They can also be done more slowly, using less energy.

The heart is the engine which keeps the body going.

Blood vessels are tubes which carry blood to every part of the body.

The lungs pass oxygen into the blood.

The heart pumps blood full of oxygen around the body

You don't need snow to learn to ski. This girl is practising on a dry ski slope. It is made of slippery fibre.

Skating and skiing build up leg **muscles**. Practice sessions may include leg bends, side bends and jumping exercises.

You need a good sense of balance to ski and skate well. You learn how to place your feet and the rest of your body, and how to move and turn.

Before a skiing session you need to loosen up. Warm-up exercises prepare your body for the ski slopes. After these exercises, you can bend and stretch more easily.

Skiing downhill

A chairlift carries skiers up to the slopes.

For about 4,500 years, people have used skis to travel over snowy ground. Skis were once long and made of heavy wood. Today, skis are shorter and lighter.

With legs bent, the skier's body makes a streamlined shape. It slips through the air more easily.

How tall are you? Your skis should be 5 to 10 centimetres longer than your height. Your ski boots must be comfortable, and carefully attached to the skis with **bindings**.

Skiing is like flying across the snow. It is one of the most exciting sports of all. Alpine skiing means skiing down hills or mountains. It includes downhill racing, where speeds can reach 200 kilometres per hour. Skiers are pulled down the slope by the force of **gravity**.

In slalom racing, skiers follow a course which zigzags around marker flags. They must turn at high speed. Do you think downhill or slalom skiing is faster?

Over the snow

Nordic skiing covers long distances cross-country, sometimes including hills. The skiers use only muscle power to push themselves forward. They cannot rely on gravity, the way a downhill skier can. Cross-country skiers may follow marked paths or trails. Sometimes they use maps to find their way.

The world's biggest Nordic skiing event is the historic race at Vasaloppet in Sweden. About 10,000 people ski over 89 kilometres.

Cross-country skiers may take long, smooth strides or short, fast steps like a skater.

Snow-shoeing and snow-boarding are popular sports.

Snowshoes are shaped like tennis racquets, and are strapped to the feet.

A snowboard is like a short surfboard that glides over the snow.

Snow-shoeing is a traditional way of crossing snowy country. Snowshoes spread the weight of the body so that it does not sink into soft snow.

Snow-boarding is a newer sport. Bindings hold the board to your feet. You balance on the board, which slides across the snow.

In the ski jump, skiing seems to turn into flying. The skier leaps without poles from a high platform.

The whole body bends forward. Why is this the best angle for moving through the air?

Skating skills

Many people skate indoors at ice rinks rather than on ponds or lakes. The ice is specially prepared. It is solid, safe, clean and smooth. Indoors, there is no wind to slow down the body.

A thin layer of water may form on the surface of the ice. This helps the skates to slide with little friction. The skater glides gracefully.

Most skates have steel blades, like knives, fixed to the bottom of the boot. Figure skates have small notches at the front of the blade. These cause friction when control is needed.

At first, just moving around on an ice rink is hard. You will often fall. Your leg muscles will ache afterwards. But with practice, you'll get used to skating.

semicircular canals

ear   inner ear

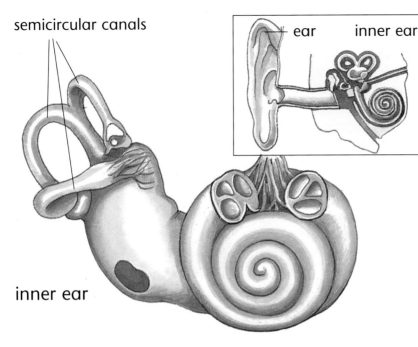

inner ear

How do skaters keep their sense of balance as they leap and swerve? The semicircular canals are tubes in the ear. They are lined with tiny hairs. As the body moves, liquid in the tubes moves the hairs. Special **cells** sense the movements and send signals to the brain.

Learning to skate well is hard work. Figure skating involves many jumps, twists and turns. It needs timing and balance. Your sense of balance comes from coiled tubes in your inner ear. These are called the semicircular canals.

Skaters may perform solo or with partners. Clothes may be simple and streamlined, or fancy and eye-catching.

Dance and speed

Ice dance brings together the **athletic** skills of skating with a feeling for music and timing, called artistic interpretation. In a competition, judges give the dancers points for all these skills.

Ice dancing may be based on the steps and patterns of stage dances. Free dance allows skaters to make

Dancing on ice is exciting and takes skill. Here the British skaters Jayne Torvill and Christopher Dean perform in an international competition.

up their own movements to the music they choose.

Speed skating is a test of strength. Skaters race over distances between 500 and 10,000 metres. They wear tight-fitting clothes and helmets, for speed and safety. They bend low to streamline their bodies. They skate with long strides, swinging their arms to push their bodies forwards.

Speed skaters travel around the rink at speeds of up to 50 kilometres per hour.

Ice hockey

Ice hockey is a fast team game played on a rink. A team has six players. Players are often taken off during the game and replaced by substitutes. The players use their hockey sticks to slide a rubber disk, called a puck, across the ice, scoring goals by shooting the puck into the net.

Ice hockey is a popular sport with young people.

A game is played in three sessions, each lasting 20 minutes.

Ice hockey is a major sport in Russia, Canada and the USA. It is becoming popular in other countries, too. Here, the Russian team plays the USA.

Players and sticks hurtle across the ice. If two players bump into each other at high speed, the collision, or **impact**, is powerful. So players must protect themselves from injuries. They wear pads on their shoulders and shins, and padded gloves and helmets.

Compare the clothes of an ice hockey player with the speed skater's outfit on page 21. What are the main differences?

helmet

shoulder pads

goal

gloves

shin pads

stick

puck

Across the ice

Curling is also played on ice. The curling stone is heavy, polished and rounded. It has a handle on top. Each player slides the stone across the ice towards a marker, or tee. The tee is fixed at the centre of a circle called the house. The nearer you get to the tee, the more points you score.

The players sweep the ice smooth in front of the curling stone. Sweeping is part of the game's skill. How does it affect the movement of the stone?

An **ice yacht** can travel at speeds of more than 200 kilometres per hour. The crew is usually one or two people. Which do you think travels faster, a light load or a heavy one?

Ice yachts have one or two sails to catch the wind. Wind power drives them across the ice. Yachts have a light frame with a backbone. A crosspiece supports two steel runners. A third runner is used as a tiller, to steer the yacht.

Ice yachts are made for slipping across the ice. Motorcycles are not! Ice speedway is a sport where motorcyclists race around a snowy track. The motorcycles have tyres with spikes in them so that they can grip the track more easily.

Tobogganing

People have used **sleds** or sledges to slide over snow for more than 8,500 years. The toboggan is a sled without runners. It was given its name long ago by Native American people. You lie on a toboggan on your front. The force of gravity helps it to slide downwards. Most children love tobogganing.

Tobogganing is fun, but be careful. There may be rocks underneath the snow. Icy bumps may throw you off course.

When toboggans and other sleds are used for sport, special courses called runs are built. The base of the run is often made of concrete, which is covered in wet snow. The snow freezes to a hard, smooth surface for a fast ride.

The world's most famous toboggan run is the Cresta, at Saint Moritz in Switzerland. It is 1,212 metres long. The run was built in 1884, when winter sports were becoming popular. It is still used today.

Super sleds

As sleds slide over snow, neither friction nor wind stops them. They overcome this **resistance**. The force of their movement is called **impetus**.

The **luge** is a streamlined sled. It carries one or two riders. They steer with their feet or a hand-held rope. A luge can travel at more than 130 kilometres per hour.

Both men and women compete in thrilling luge races at the Winter Olympics. The Winter Olympics started in 1924. They are held every four years.

This two-person bobsleigh shoots down the run, gathering speed. The second rider bends forward to make the bobsleigh as streamlined as possible.

The most streamlined sleds are the bobsleighs. They are shaped like long bullets. Bobsleighs can hold teams of two or four. The riders take a running start, jump in and hurtle down runs of 1,500 metres. The course has steep banks and hairpin bends. As the bobsleigh turns a corner, it tilts at an angle.

Riders steer bobsleighs with a wheel or with ropes. These sleighs have two double sets of runners.

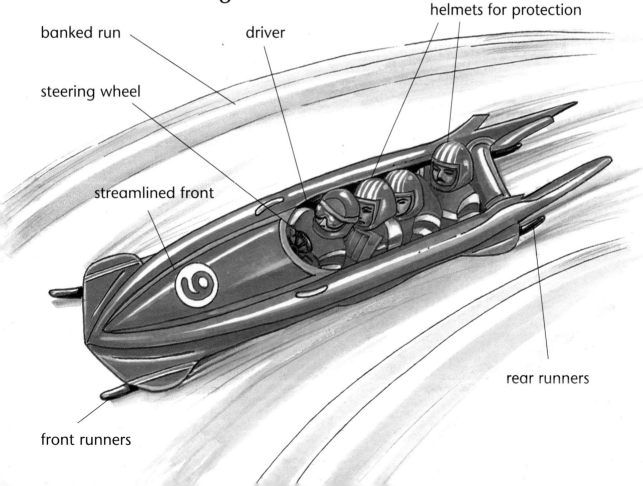

banked run

driver

helmets for protection

steering wheel

streamlined front

rear runners

front runners

Words we use

artificial something that is not natural, often made from chemicals

athletic using fitness and strength

avalanche a large mass of sliding snow

bindings metal or plastic fasteners that hold boots on skis and snowboards

cells the tiny structures that make up our bodies

crystals the shapes formed inside something when it changes from a liquid to a solid

curling a team ice sport, which is similar to bowling

energy the power to carry out an action or movement

freeze to turn a liquid to a solid at a low temperature

friction the rubbing of one surface against another

frostbite damage to the fingers, toes or other parts of the body, caused by the cold

gravity a force which pulls objects or people towards the ground

hail showers of small balls of ice

hypothermia the state when the body reaches a dangerously low temperature

ice yacht a sail-powered frame with runners

impact the force of two objects hitting each other

impetus the force that moves something or the force something has when it moves

liquid a substance that runs or flows

luge a fast sporting sled, for drivers who are sitting or lying down

muscles fibres in the body that can move other parts of the body, such as bones

oxygen a gas found in air and water

resistance the ability to stop or slow down the movement of someone or something

runner a strip of wood, steel or other material designed to slide across snow or ice

scale a way something is divided up to measure it

skis thin pieces of wood, metal or plastic, fixed under boots

sled or **sledge** a platform on runners

sleet a mixture of snow and rain

sleigh a horse-drawn carriage with runners instead of wheels

solid something that is firm or hard

streamlined shaped to move through air or water easily

sun-block cream which protects the skin by blocking out some of the sun's harmful rays

temperature how hot or cold something is. It is measured in degrees Fahrenheit or Celsius.

thermometer an instrument for measuring how hot or cold something is

vapour a liquid that has turned into a gas, like steam from a kettle

Index